Smart About Sports

Meet the Cowboys

By
Mike Kennedy
with Mark Stewart

Norwood House Press

Norwood House Press, P.O. Box 316598, Chicago, Illinois 60631

For information regarding Norwood House Press,
please visit our website at: www.norwoodhousepress.com or call 866-565-2900.

Photo Credits:
Associated Press (4, 22), Getty Images (7, 8, 12, 13, 15, 16, 18, 20, 21, 23).
Cover Photos:
Top Left: The Upper Deck Company; Top Right: James D. Smith/Icon SMI;
Bottom Left: James D. Smith/Icon SMI; Bottom Right: Topps, Inc.
The football memorabilia photographed for this book is part of the authors' collection:
Page 6) Don Meredith, Philadelphia Gum Company, Page 10) Bob Lilly, Mel Renfro & Randy White: Topps, Inc.;
Roger Staubach: Crane Potato Chips,Page 11) Michael Irvin & Troy Aikman: Fleer Corp.; Emmitt Smith: Topps, Inc.;
DeMarcus Ware: The Upper Deck Company.
Special thanks to Topps, Inc.

Editor: Brian Fitzgerald
Designer: Ron Jaffe
Project Management: Black Book Partners, LLC.
Editorial Production: Jessica McCulloch

Library of Congress Cataloging-in-Publication Data

Kennedy, Mike.
Meet the Cowboys / by Mike Kennedy with Mark Stewart.
p. cm. -- (Smart about sports)
Includes bibliographical references and index.
Summary: "An introductory look at the Dallas Cowboys football team. Includes a brief history, facts, photos, records, glossary, and fun activities"--Provided by publisher.
ISBN-13: 978-1-59953-395-7 (library edition : alk. paper)
ISBN-10: 1-59953-395-2 (library edition : alk. paper)
1. Dallas Cowboys (Football team)--History--Juvenile literature. I. Stewart, Mark. II. Title.
GV956.D3K46 2011
796.332'64097642812--dc22

2010008499

Manufactured in the United States of America in North Mankato, Minnesota.
172R—022011

Contents

Words in **bold type** are defined on page 24.

Good job! The Cowboys hug Emmitt Smith (#22) after a score.

The Dallas Cowboys

The Dallas Cowboys are
called America's Team.
Fans all over the country
root for them. The players
are proud to be Cowboys.
They always play hard.

Once Upon a Time

The Cowboys joined the National Football League (NFL) in 1960. Coach Tom Landry made them a winning team.

The Cowboys have always put great players on the field. Don Meredith and Bob Hayes were two of the best.

Bob Hayes leaps high
to catch a pass.

Fans watch the huge video screen high above the field.

At the Stadium

The Cowboys play their home games at Cowboys Stadium. It holds more than 100,000 people. A large video screen hangs over the field. It shows the whole game in high definition.

Shoe Box

The cards on these pages belong to the authors. They show some of the best Cowboys ever.

Bob Lilly

Defensive Lineman

• 1961–1974

Bob Lilly was the star of the team's defense.

Mel Renfro

Defensive Back

• 1964–1977

Mel Renfro made the **Pro Bowl** 10 years in a row.

Roger Staubach

Quarterback

• 1969–1979

Roger Staubach had a strong arm and quick feet. He was also a great leader.

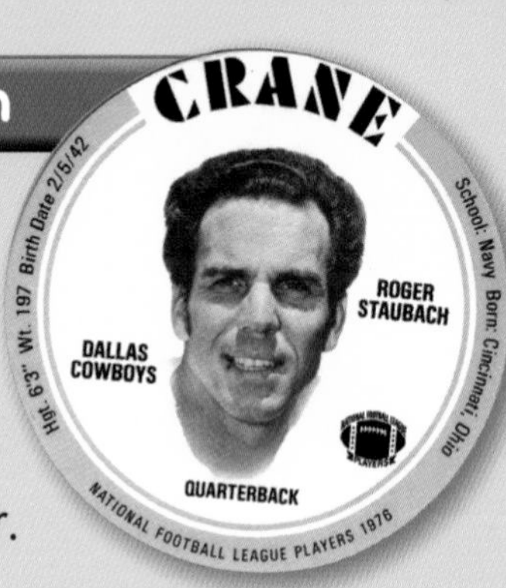

Randy White

Defensive Lineman

• 1975–1988

Randy White was very hard to block. He made tackles all over the field.

Michael Irvin

Receiver • 1988–1999
Michael Irvin used his size and strength to catch passes.

Troy Aikman

Quarterback • 1989–2000
Troy Aikman led the Cowboys to three **Super Bowl** wins.

Emmitt Smith

Running Back • 1990–2002
Emmitt Smith was small. But he ran with the heart of a giant.

DeMarcus Ware

Linebacker • 2005–
DeMarcus Ware loved to tackle quarterbacks before they passed.

ABC's of Football

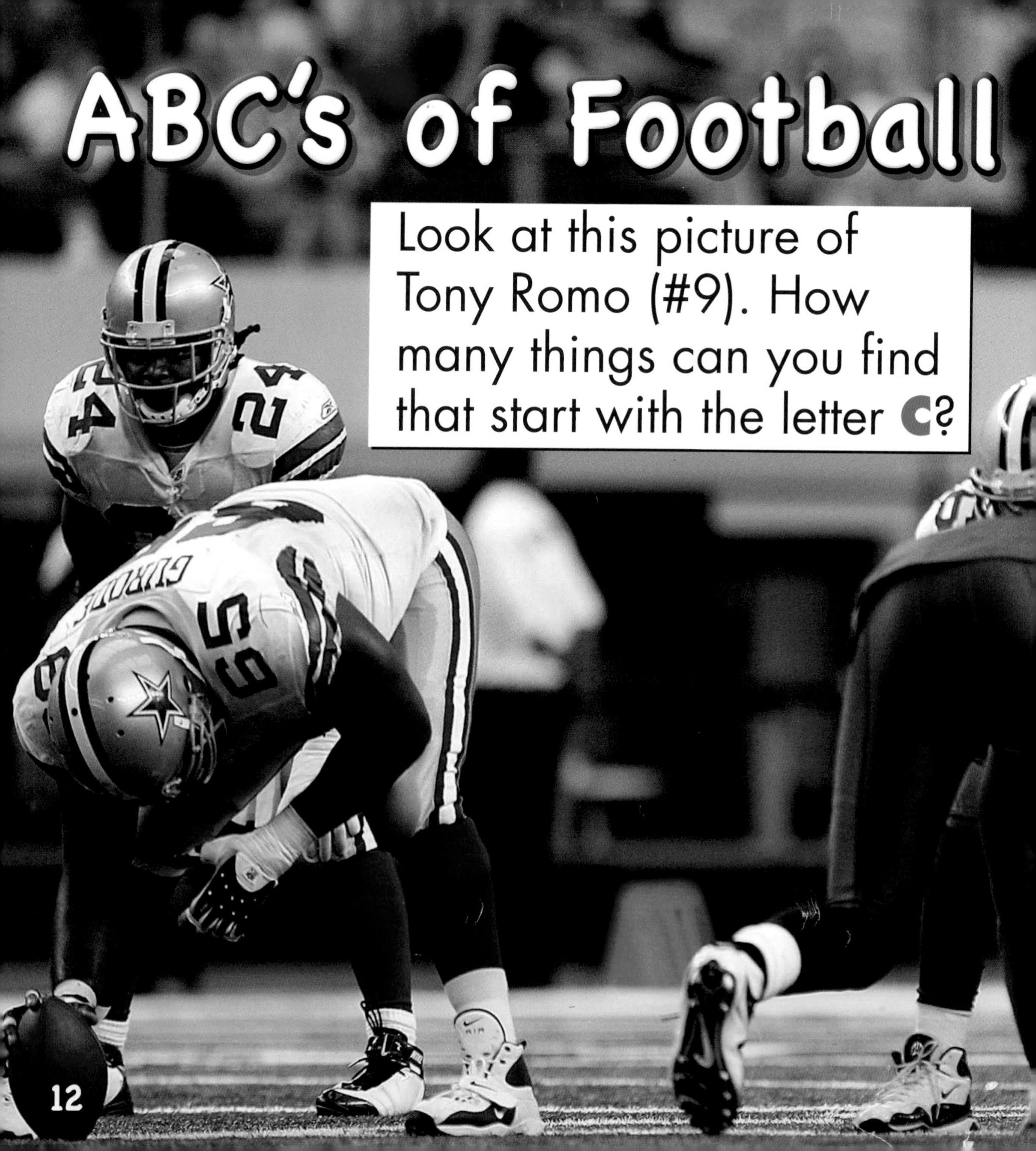

Look at this picture of Tony Romo (#9). How many things can you find that start with the letter C?

See page 23
for answer.

Brain Games

Here is a poem about a famous Cowboy:

Tacklers never had fun
When the Cowboys wanted to run.
The ball went to Tony,
Who ran like a pony.
He shined like a ray of the sun.

Guess which one of these facts is **TRUE**:

- *Tony Dorsett once scored on a 99-**yard** run.*
- *Tony was very slow.*

See page 23 for answer.

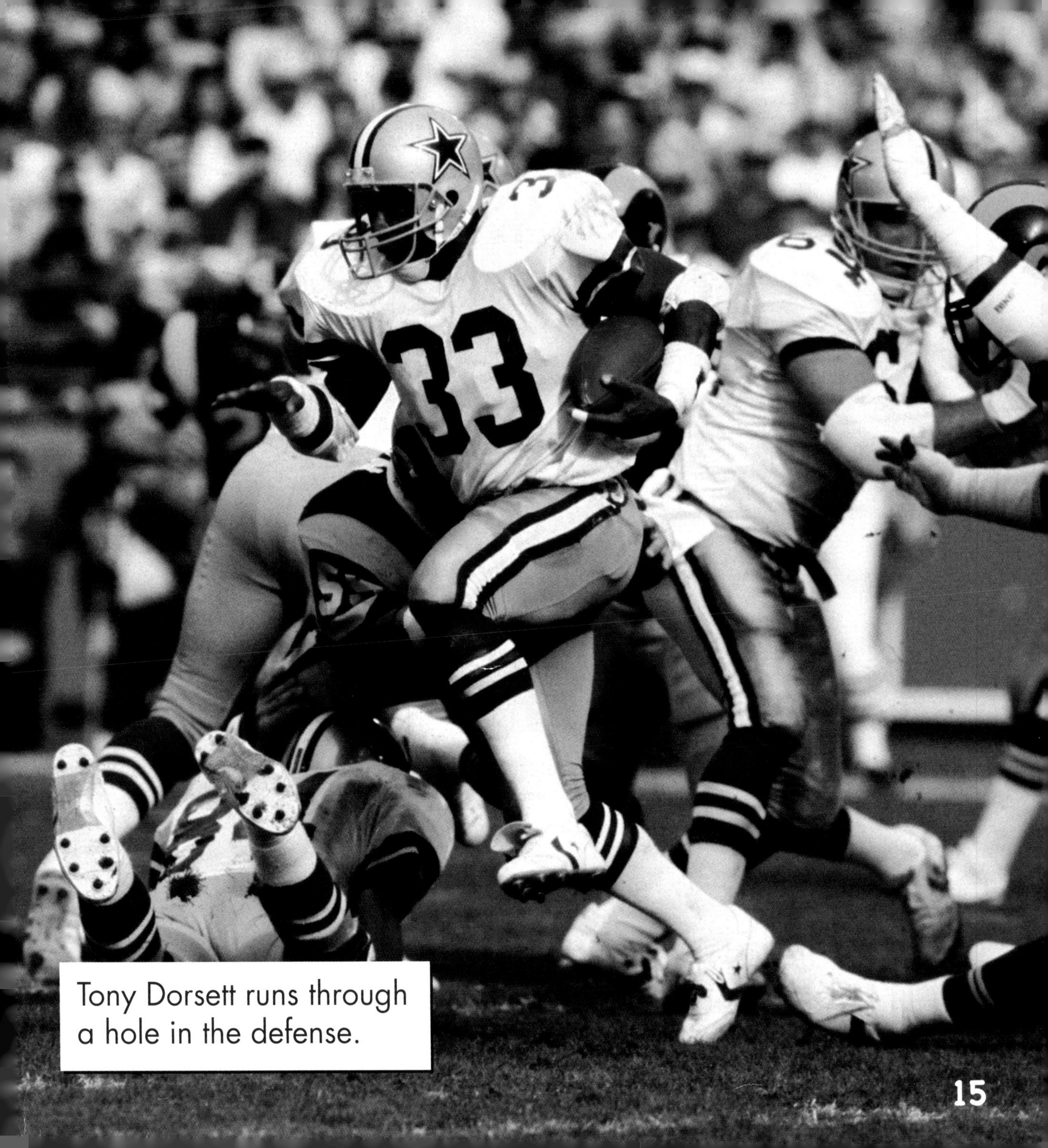

Tony Dorsett runs through a hole in the defense.

Fans love Rowdy and the Dallas Cowboys Cheerleaders.

Fun on the Field

Cowboys games are a lot of fun. Fans love the team's mascot. His name is Rowdy. Fans also like to watch the Dallas Cowboys Cheerleaders.

On the Map

The Cowboys call Dallas, Texas home. The players come from all over the world. These Cowboys played in the Pro Bowl. Match each with the place he was born:

1. **Chuck Howley • Pro Bowl: 1965–1969 & 1971**
   Wheeling, West Virginia
2. **Calvin Hill • Pro Bowl: 1969 & 1972–1974**
   Baltimore, Maryland
3. **Drew Pearson • Pro Bowl: 1974, 1976 & 1977**
   South River, New Jersey
4. **Efren Herrera • Pro Bowl: 1977**
   Guadalajara, Mexico
5. **Ed "Too Tall" Jones • Pro Bowl: 1981–1983**
   Jackson, Tennessee

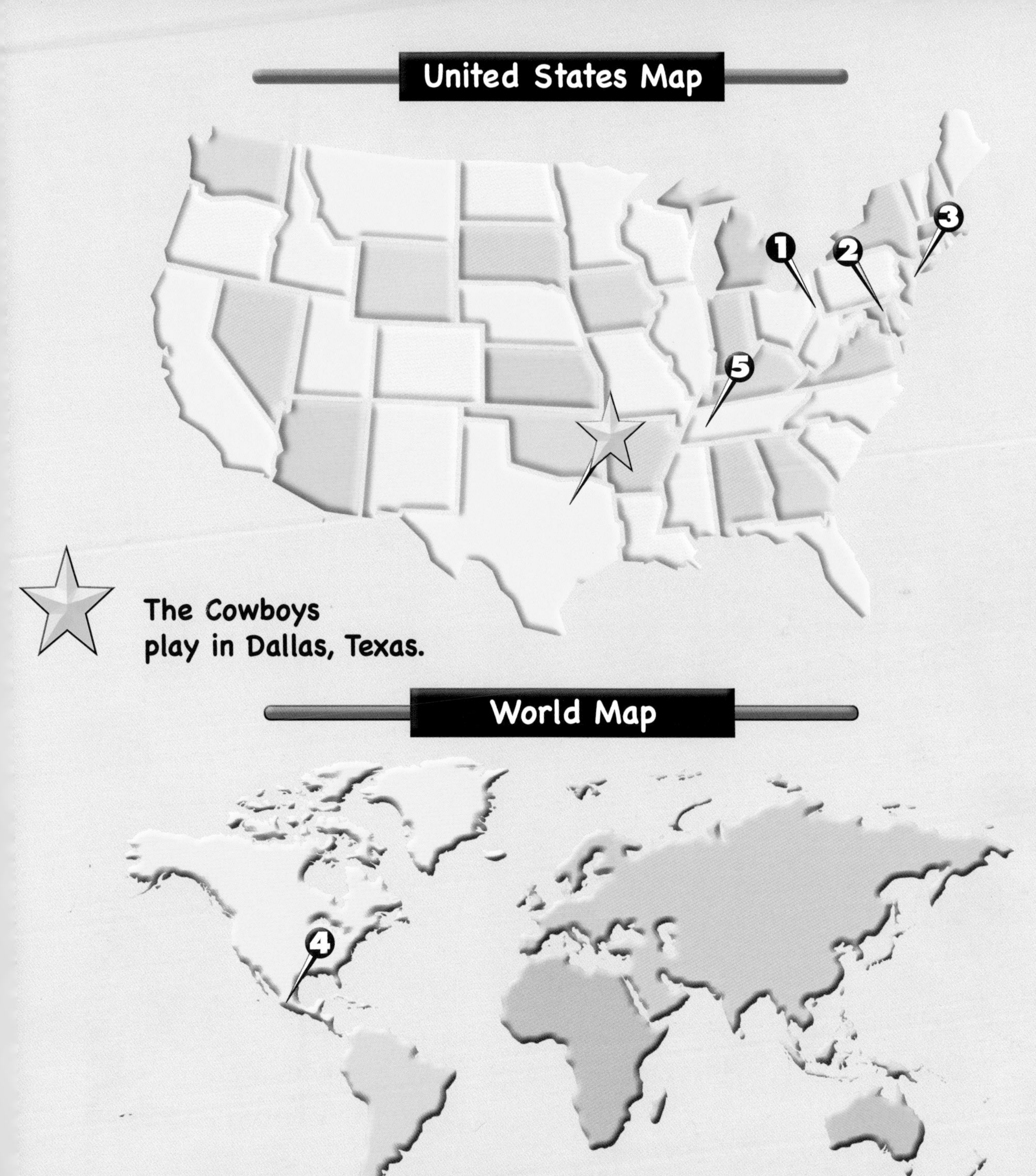
United States Map
1
2
3
5
The Cowboys
play in Dallas, Texas.
World Map
4

What's in the Locker?

The Cowboys like to wear a white jersey for every game. The players think this brings them good luck.

Jason Witten wears the team's favorite uniform.

Sometimes, the Cowboys wear a blue uniform and white helmet. For most games, they wear a silver helmet with a blue star. The star is the Star of Texas.

Felix Jones wears the team's blue jersey and white helmet.

We Won!

The Cowboys are one of the NFL's best teams. They play tough defense. They score lots of points. From 1971 to 1995, the Cowboys won the Super Bowl five times.

Jimmy Johnson and Troy Aikman hug after their win in Super Bowl 28.

Record Book

These Cowboys stars set team records.

Running Back	Record	Year
Emmitt Smith	1,773 yards	1995
Emmitt Smith	25 **touchdowns**	1995

Quarterback/Receiver	Record	Year
Bob Hayes	26.1 yards per catch	1970
Michael Irvin	111 catches	1995
Terrell Owens	15 touchdown catches	2007
Tony Romo	36 touchdown passes	2007

Answer for ABC's of Football

Here are some words in the picture that start with **C**:
Chin Strap, Cleats, Cowboys Uniform.
Did you find any others?

Answer for Brain Games

The first fact is true. Tony Dorsett ran for a 99-yard touchdown in 1983. He was a very fast runner.

Football Words

PRO BOWL
A special game played between the NFL's top stars.

SUPER BOWL
The game that decides the champion of the NFL.

TOUCHDOWNS
Scoring plays worth six points.

YARD
A yard is a distance of three feet. A football field is 100 yards long from goal line to goal line.

Index

Photos are on **bold** numbered pages.

About the Cowboys

Learn more about the Cowboys at www.dallascowboys.com

Learn more about football at www.profootballhof.com